1) Start with three O's.

2) Add two dots, two short lines…

3) and two loops.

4) Draw three C's…

5) seven angles…

6) and sixteen little lines.

Bonjour!

Où est le ketchup?

Oui, oui!

7) Add two more flies flying the opposite way.

# FRENCH FLIES

Are French fries French? In France they are called pommes frites, but some people say they were first made in Belgium. Wherever they come from, these potato sticks are definitely fried (in boiling oil) not just once, but twice, to make them crispy outside and moist inside.

1) Start with three curves.

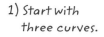

2) Add a skinny loop . . .

3) and seven more curves.

4) Draw two long curves down . . .

5) and connect with an O.

6) Attach a loop at the bottom . . .

7) and put a cherry on top!

# MICE CREAM SUNDAE

I scream, you scream, we all scream for ice cream — and not just on Sunday! Ice cream has been a treat for more than a thousand years, first made in China.

1) Draw spaghetti with four groups of three curves.

2) Draw a lot more spaghetti.

3) Put a plate under it...

4) and tomato sauce on top.

# SPAGHETTI AND MOTHBALLS

Spaghetti is slippery and sloppy and silly! What's the silliest way to eat spaghetti? Start at one end and slurp without stopping. A safer way to eat spaghetti is to slowly twirl a few strands around your fork.

5) Make moths with two loops...

6) and three loops...

7) and four loops.

8) Turn the moths into mothballs.

1) Draw a loop.

2) Add ten short curves.

3) Put a double curve around . . .

4) and two lines down.

5) Draw three horizontal curves . . .

6) and seven vertical ones.

# STRAWBERRY MILK SNAKE

There really are milk snakes but they don't drink milk. They hang around cow barns because they're looking for mice.

1) Draw two curves.

2) Add an oval and an angle.

3) Draw two squiggle hands ...

4) and three squiggle curves.

5) Draw ten curves and four dots.

6) Add short furry lines.

7) Draw seven squiggle lines...

8) and four loopy feet.

# MACARONI AND CHIMPANZEES

Strings, ribbons, shells, tubes, bowties, stars, spirals, stars, even letters of the alphabet—pasta comes in lots of different shapes. So why is macaroni hollow and curved like an elbow? It's in the sauce! Elbow macaroni is a great shape to hold creamy cheese sauce.

# COLLIE FLOWER

Cauliflower is one flower that belongs on your plate, not in a vase!

1) Draw two eyes, a T nose . . .

2) and pointy ears.

3) Add four curves to smile.

4) Use short lines to draw fur . . .

5) more lines . . .

6) and more.

7) Draw four squiggly leaves.

1) Draw a tiny heart.

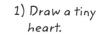

2) Add nine more flying around.

3) Draw a double-hooked line.

4) Attach a long squared loop.

5) Draw a half circle . . .

6) and decorate your salad bowl with your favorite fruit.

# FRUIT FLY SALAD

Fruit flies are small – just 1/2 inch long – but numerous. There are over 4,500 different kinds of fruit flies and they all love fruit salad.

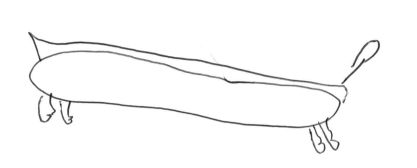

1) Draw a long loop.

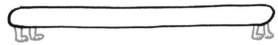

2) Add four paws.

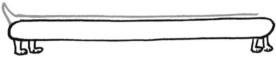

3) Make a long line with a tail . . .

4) and attach an ear, eye, nose, and snout.

# FOOT-LONG HOT DOG

Put a sausage in a bun, serve it hot, and you'll have a dog that loves cat-shup!

5) Add catsup!

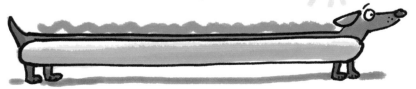

1) Draw two pairs of curves.

2) Connect with four lines and add two angles.

3) Draw two long lines and connect with two curves.

4) Add eyes, noses, whiskers . . .

5) ears . . .

6) and tails!

# CAT-SHUP
## AND
# MOUSE-TARD

Here's a cat and mouse that get along great together – especially on a dog!

1) Draw a flat, curved C.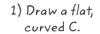

2) Add three curves . . .

3) and four more curves.

4) Attach three squiggles.

5) Put an oval and a curve underneath . . .

6) and a half circle above.

# HUMMINGBURGER

Hummingbirds fly up, down, sideways, forwards, and backwards! They can hover in mid-air and speed dive at 60 miles per hour. These tiny birds fly this fast and fancy by beating their wings 70 times per second. To keep up their strength, they need to eat — up to three times their body weight in flower nectar plus a few bugs for protein.

7) Now try to catch that hummingburger in a bun.

1) Draw a half-circle.

2) Add two bunny ears . . .

3) eyes, nose, and whiskers.

4) Put a hamburger on a
   plate with four curves.

5) Don't forget the lettuce . . .

# HAMBURGER BUNNY

The first burger on a bun was
made by Mr. and Mrs. Oscar Weber
Bilby of Tulsa, Oklahoma in 1891.
Mr. Bilby grilled the burgers and
Mrs. Bilby baked the buns. Since
then billions of burgers on buns
have been made.

6) or the
   carrot juice.

1) Draw a curlicue.

2) Add two little loops and a curve.

3) Attach an O and a squiggly C.

4) Put ten curves inside . . .

5) and put the python in a dish.

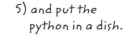

## DEEP DISH APPLE PYTHON

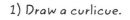

You need a deep dish to hold a python — some are nearly 20 feet long.

6) Serve with ice cream. Pythons love ice cream.

VANILLA

1) Draw three leaf shapes.

2) Add two dots and three curves.

3) Draw a puffy cloud . . .

4) and two V's.

5) Connect with a curve . . .

6) add four angles . . .

7) and loopy feet.

# BLUEBERRY PUFFIN

If you invite a puffin to breakfast, don't bother fixing anything but fish. It's best to serve the fish in your bathtub or better yet, swimming pool, filled with very cold water. Make sure that there's plenty of fish and don't be surprised if the puffin dives in, catches all the fish in its mouth underwater, and then flies off to eat somewhere else.

# CHOCOLATE MOOSE

Chocolate starts from a small seed. The seed pods of the cacao tree are fermented, dried, roasted, ground, refined, heated, and mixed with sugar to make deliciously sweet chocolate treats, including cakes, candies, kisses, and mousse (the dessert, not the critter).

1) Draw two O's and two leaf shapes.

2) Add three curves.

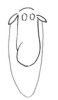

3) Attach a big U . . .

4) three lines . . .

5) and a soft triangle.

6) Make a big loopy antler . . .

7) and another one.

1) Draw a grape shape.

2) Add a curve around.

3) Make two eyes under a curve and a smile.

4) Draw fur lines and nostrils . . .

5) and four squiggly curves down.

6) Add two squiggly lines and curvy fingers.

7) Draw more fur lines.

8) Add a bunch of purple Great GrApes!

# THE GREAT GRAPE

Is it the world's only purple primate or the world's furriest fruit? In the real world, both apes and grapes hang out in bunches.

1) Draw a weird G.

2) Add four curves.

3) Draw two round eyes and 26 pointy teeth.

4) Draw one squiggly curve and one smooth curve.

5) Add two 2's, and four V's.

6) Make loopy fingers and feet . . .

7) and a curvy tail.

8) Put your T-Rex between two slices of bread, lettuce, and bacon.

## BLT-REX

If you were a T-Rex, you would be able to take a 500-lb. bite out of a BLT sandwich! That's a mouthful!

1) Draw an egg shape.

2) Add two dotted eyes . . .

3) and a curvy C.

4) Draw three long U's . . .

5) and seven curves.

6) Make three V's, one upside down

7) Add another U and a short line.

# GRASSHOPSICLE

Grasshoppers don't need any help to hop. With their strong hind legs they can jump twenty times their body length — which is like a 4-foot tall kid jumping from one end of a basketball court to the other.

1) Draw four circles.

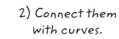

2) Connect them with curves.

3) Draw three ovals.

4) Add three curves.

5) Put your panda on a giant plate.

6) Add tons of syrup and butter.

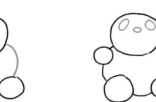

# GIANT PANDACAKES

Giant pandas are big — up to 250 pounds. In the wild the only thing they eat is bamboo, up to 40 pounds of bamboo leaves, shoots, and stems every day — without syrup or butter.

1) Draw two curves...

2) and two more curves.

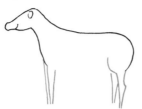

3) Add five straight and two curvy vertical lines . . .

4) and one horizontal line.

5) Draw hooves, ears, mane, and tail.

6) Add the pepperoni.

# PEPPERONI ZEBRA

Of course you'll never see a Pepperoni Zebra, but why are zebras striped instead of spotted? Some scientists think that a zebra's stripes blend not only with the tall grass, but also with other zebras. That confuses lions looking for their next meal. Since lions are color-blind, it doesn't matter if the stripes are green and blue, or black and white.

# SALAMANDERWICH

Hundreds of years ago, people used big pieces of stale bread as plates, putting meat and other food on top. If they were still hungry after eating the meat, they'd eat their plates. It just took another "plate" on top to make a sandwich, a meal you can pick up with your hands.

1) Draw half a cloud.

2) Put a salamander head, tail, and feet under it.

3) Add lettuce and a big curve.

4) Put a pickle on top.

1) Draw two curves.

2) Connect the ends with angles.

3) Draw eight curves and a T.

4) Attach four vertical lines.

5) Connect the ends with a curve and paws.

6) Add black spots.

# SALT AND LEOPARD

Salt is more than a flavor. It helps our bodies run smoothly and is found in our blood, sweat, and tears. People have been harvesting salt — and making other things from it — for thousands of years. Before refrigerators, it was used to preserve food, and today it has over 14,000 uses.

1) Start with five small curves.

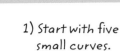

2) Add six more curves . . .

3) and four more curves.

4) Draw five eyes, three noses, one ear, and one smile.

5) Make stripes and whiskers . . .

6) and wiggly tails.

# CHOCOLATE CHIPMUNK COOKIES

Don't stuff your face — unless you're a chipmunk! Chipmunks stuff nuts, berries, and seeds into their cheeks to carry back to their nests to store for winter.

7) Add more cookies and put them on a plate!

1) Draw three O's . . .

2) and six eyes.

3) Attach six striped U's.

4) Draw three lines, three V's . . .

5) and three pairs of loopy wings.

6) Use short lines for legs and antennae . . .

7) and grill on bread.

# GRILLED BEES

Isn't it sweet? Bees make enough honey for themselves to eat during the winter and more — so we humans can enjoy it all year round.

1) Draw a squiggly O and a weird W.

2) Add two eyes and a smile.

3) Draw four V's and four curves . . .

4) squiggly ears and loopy fingers.

5) Make a ring...

6) and put the koala in a bowl.

KOALA SLAW

Koalas are sometimes called bears, but they're actually marsupials and, like kangaroos, they carry their young in a pouch. You'll never find koalas eating your cole slaw because they only eat eucalyptus leaves, and cole slaw is made from cabbage.

1) Start with a cherry on top.

2) Add a blob . . .

3) and two scoops.

4) Draw two spoons . . .

5) two dots, three curves, and a weird loop.

6) Make a boat of two big curves.

# BANANA SLUG SPLIT

Don't eat that banana . . . it's a slug! A banana slug looks like a banana except that it's slimy and slow and has two eyes on stalks at the top of its head.

1) Draw a T, an O, and a U.

2) Add ten curves . . .

3) five squiggles and two dots.

4) Make a big curve and attach a curvy tail.

5) Add four legs with hooves.

6) Put the bull on a bun.

7) Put the bun on a plate.

8) Put the plate on a table.

## BULL—ONEY SANDWICH

No baloney! Baloney first came from Bologna in Italy, where it's called mortadella.

1) Draw a squiggle and a J.

2) Add three squiggles . . .

3) two angles . . .

4) and three lines.

5) Draw two curvy curves . . .

6) and five squiggly curves.

7) Add loopy paws . . .

8) bear eyes and nose and guitar head.

9) Make another black bear jammin'!

# BLACK BEARY JAM

Black bears love blackberries — and blueberries, raspberries, dewberries, cranberries, soapberries, crowberries, strawberries, and gooseberries. Bears love berries so much that sometimes they eat the leaves and stems, too!

1) Draw three curls.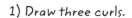

2) Add four eyes.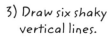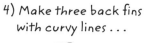

3) Draw six shaky vertical lines.

4) Make three back fins with curvy lines . . .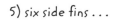

5) six side fins . . .

  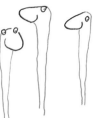

6) and three tail fins.

# FISH STICKS

Believe it or not, there are fish that walk and they don't need walking sticks to help them. The mudskipper uses its pectoral, or side fins, not only to walk on land, but also to climb trees.

1) Draw a long horizontal loop.

2) Add three horizontal lines . . .
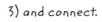

3) and connect.
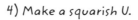

4) Make a squarish U.
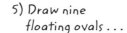

5) Draw nine floating ovals . . .

6) with colored squiggles underneath.

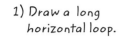 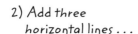

## JELLYFISH BEANS

Jellyfish live under the sea, and jelly beans are out of this world! Or at least they were in 1983 when then President Reagan put his favorite candy into orbit aboard the space shuttle Challenger.

1) Start with two small eyes and a big nose.

2) Add three squiggly curves . . .

3) and two squiggly horizontal lines.

4) Draw six curves and a squiggle.

5) Make four skinny legs.

6) Design your own package.

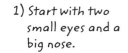
# GRANOLA BOAR

Granola bars are made from pressed granola which is made from baked rolled oats which are made from flattened oat groats which are made from dehulled grains of oat.

# PEAR-ROT

Polly may want more than a cracker if she tries to say: *A pair of parrots pared a pair of pears purely for pleasure.*

Can you say that sentence really fast five times?

1) Start with a pear.

2) Add two curvy C's for a beak . . .

3) and five curvy C's for feet.

4) Draw an eye and a curve.

5) Add a weird W . . .

6) and rows of squiggles.

7) Make another weird W.

8) Put your Pear-rot in a pear tree!